The Kern Alphabet Book

written and illustrated by

Donna Kern

COVE PRESS

An imprint of
U.S. GAMES SYSTEMS, INC.
179 Ludlow Street
Stamford, CT 06902 USA

Bite or bake or juggle or grapple,

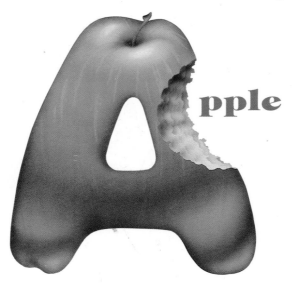pple

A is for anything you can do with an Apple.

Beads and toys and colorful socks,

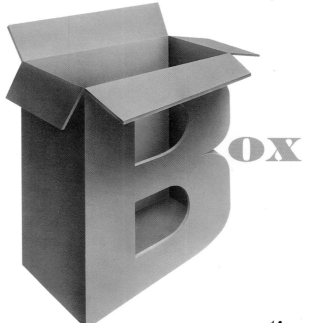

Box

B is for things you can put in a Box.

A house or a tree or a trumpet to play on.

rayon

C is for things you can draw with a Crayon.

Sparkling like water on a tropical island,

Diamond

D is for donning a dazzling Diamond.

Keep the caviar, forget the frogs' legs,

gg

E is for eating everyday Eggs.

Wave and wag, zig and zag,

lag

F is for flying a fabulous Flag.

I hoped for a pet and then made a wish,

Goldfish

G is for getting a great new Goldfish.

A hole in the wall is home for a mouse,

ouse

H is for having my own little House.

Stacked up like cubes or blocks or dice,

ce

I is for sculptures built out of Ice.

Bounce the red ball, get ready to catch,

Jacks

J is for joyously picking up Jacks.

Open and close and open with ease,

Keys

K is for keeping things locked up with Keys.

Creatures with claws are not always monsters,

obster

L is for liking all loveable Lobsters.

Running around different ways in a daze,

aze

M is for a mouse who gets lost in a Maze.

Squiggly and wiggly like scribbling doodles,

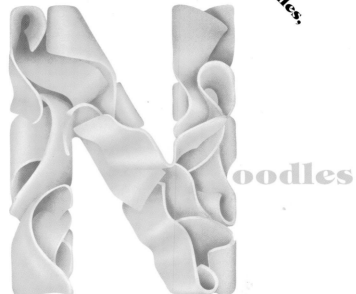

oodles

N is for oodles and boodles of Noodles.

Juice in your eye will make you cringe,

range

O is for squeezing the pulp from an Orange.

Pictures or poems or letters you stencil,

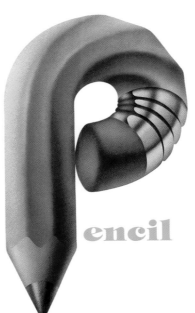

Pencil

P is for things you can draw with a Pencil.

Square by square, a patchwork we built,

Quilt

Q is for sewing and stitching a Quilt.

A gift is a secret surprise 'til it's given,

Ribbon

R is for presents wrapped in red Ribbon.

It looks like a stallion, but tiny of course,

eahorse

S is for seeing a squiggly Seahorse.

Looking as far as the eye can see,

ree

T is for climbing to the top of a Tree.

Standing in the rain I saw a fella,

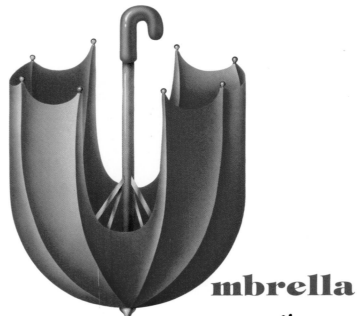

mbrella

U is for offering to share my Umbrella.

Violets or vines, or ivy like lace,

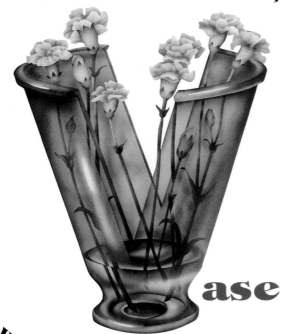

ase

V is for various flowers in a Vase.

When surfing and sailing you have to be brave,

Waves

W is for riding the crest of a Wave.

Marching in time or playing alone,

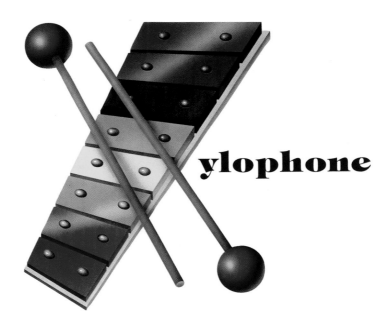

ylophone

X is for tapping a toy Xylophone.

To knit or knot or mend or darn,

Yarn

Y is for yards and yards of Yarn.

Button or fasten or close with a clipper,

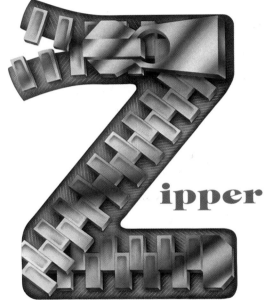

Zipper

Z is for zipping it up with a Zipper.

Library of Congress Cataloging-in-Publication Data
Kern, Donna.
The Kern alphabet book/written and illustrated by Donna Kern.
    p.   cm.
Summary: Rhyming text and illustrations present the letters of the
alphabet, from "A" is for anything you can do with an Apple" to
"Z is for zipping it up with a zipper."
ISBN 1-57281-099-8 (hardcover)
1. English language–Alphabet–Juvenile literature.
[1. Alphabet.]   I. Title
PE1155.K47   1998
428.1–dc21
[E]   98-12911
CIP
AC

Printed in Hong Kong

99 10 9 8 7 6 5 4 3 2 1

An imprint of
U.S. GAMES SYSTEMS, INC.
179 Ludlow Street
Stamford, CT 06902 USA